Notes

from

Your

Therapist

Notes from Your Therapist

A book about feelings

ALLYSON DINNEEN

bluebird
books for life

First published 2021 by Houghton Mifflin Harcourt

First published in the UK 2021 by Bluebird
an imprint of Pan Macmillan
The Smithson, 6 Briset Street, London, EC1M 5NR
EU representative: Macmillan Publishers Ireland Ltd, Mallard Lodge,
Lansdowne Village, Dublin 4
Associated companies throughout the world
www.panmacmillan.com

ISBN 978-1-5290-7396-6

Pan Macmillan does not have any control over, or any responsibility for,
any author or third-party websites referred to in or on this book.

9 8 7 6 5 4 3 2 1

A CIP catalogue record for this book is available from the British Library.

Book design by Tai Blanche

Printed and Bound in Italy

Visit www.panmacmillan.com to read more about all our books and to buy them. You will
also find features, author interviews and news of any author events, and you can sign
up for e-newsletters so that you're always first to hear about our new releases.

For Patricia and Rafe

Introduction

Here is a book about feelings.

I grew up on a farm, and in those days I didn't know anyone who talked about sadness, regret, loss, or death. When I was a little girl, my mother died when her plane crashed. One day she was right there, and the next moment she was gone. No one ever mentioned her again. We were supposed to silently close the door like nothing had happened. Forget all about pain or loss or tragedy, including people you loved.

You definitely didn't talk about feelings.

It was hard to know what to do as a kid, surrounded by unhappy, destructive, troubled adults. I was constantly caught in their crossfire of unspoken anger and sorrow. So I did the only thing I could think of to do. Which was hide.

In my closet with my books to read about other people's

Mostly I just wanted to tell the truth as I saw it.

lives. Or disappearing into the woods for hours at a time, pretending to be a lost orphan.

One Christmas morning when I was eight, I got a diary with a gold lock and key. And that's when I began taking notes.

I wrote down all the things no one talked about. And tried to make sense of adults and what they did. I wanted to daydream and understand life and myself.

Mostly I just wanted to tell the truth as I saw it.

Many years later, after life and kids and some interesting adventures, I became a professional at conversations about feelings and life—I became a therapist. My passion for writing and for talking about emotions and hard things had never stopped.

Happy in life and my new career, I unexpectedly fell in love. I wasn't planning for that. But I was even less ready when, three years later, right after we had a new baby, my beloved husband died in an accident.

I didn't think I could ever recover.

The only thing I knew for sure was that I wouldn't raise our daughter in the kind of silence I'd grown up in. And that's about all I had to go on to survive.

I definitely didn't think I would ever be a therapist again. What did I have left to give?

But as the years passed, life started coming back to me. I began writing again to process my grief, and I began to see some clients. One day, on a whim, I posted something I wrote on Instagram. There was no plan. I didn't tell anyone. I wasn't even sure if it was an okay thing to do. I just wanted to be the person I had needed as a kid: someone who wasn't too afraid to talk about feelings or about hard things, someone who would let me tell the truth as I saw it. Quietly at first, people shared with their friends what I wrote about emotions, relationships, and life. And that was the beginning of Notes from Your Therapist.

Apparently it's okay to talk about hard things.

This is also a book about flying. And by flying, I mean being true to yourself. Sometimes no one wants you to fly, not even the people you love most. But you gotta fly.

I wrote this book for the other people who think they have to hide their wish to fly.

If that's you, I don't want you to think you're the only one.

When I grew up
you were supposed to
do what you were told &
not ask questions.

But I had questions.

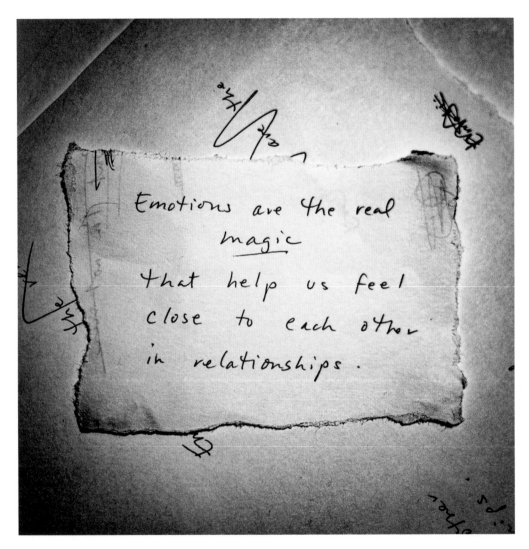

Human beings are
a species evolved for
secure connection
with others —
that's just human biology +
neuroscience.

But some of us wonder
if we can feel secure
without being <u>abandoned</u>

+

some of us wonder
if we can feel secure
without being <u>overwhelmed</u>.
Some of us
a little of both.

You don't have to
"get over"
your feelings.

Why shouldn't they
take as long as
they take?

So often
we're not allowed to
feel upset
— even for a minute —

without the world
rushing us to
Do something
about it.

But why can't I
feel upset?

Good emotion skills means
understanding that
These 2 things are not the same

feeling   acting out

LIFE GOALS

Practice staying in
uncomfortable conversations
with people I love —
even though I want to
run away.

Probably my

entire relationship

Feelings
are signals sent
from your body's
nervous system
about your
physical + emotional
state :

to tell you
how you're doing
+
what you need.

You're meant
to notice them.

Needing others is
so BASIC to our
human biology that
teaching people
n<u>ot</u> to need others
is teaching trauma.

And the major tool
for that is ~~$~~
Shame.

When family, school +
society put
so much emphasis on
being perfect, strong,
happy + well-adjusted –

no surprise we
conclude
we have to be all
those things to be loved.
And grow up never knowing
that to be vulnerable,
messy, human
is lovable.

You might not WA<u>NT</u>
to feel needy.
But your nervous system
is extremely evolved to
d<u>ri</u>ve you
to seek safe
emotional connection
with others —
and it has millions
of years of a
head start
on your wish to be
above that.

the Importance of
Feelings in
Relationships –

If no one knows
how I feel about

myself / life /
where I've been /
what I need . . .

nobody actually

knows me.

How else are you
going to learn how
to handle conflict +
calmly disagree if
you were never
allowed to do that
growing up?

Of course you're scared.

It takes practice.

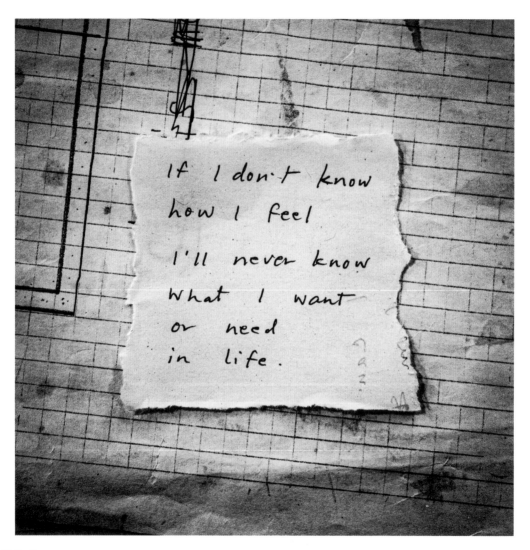

[26] How to know how you feel

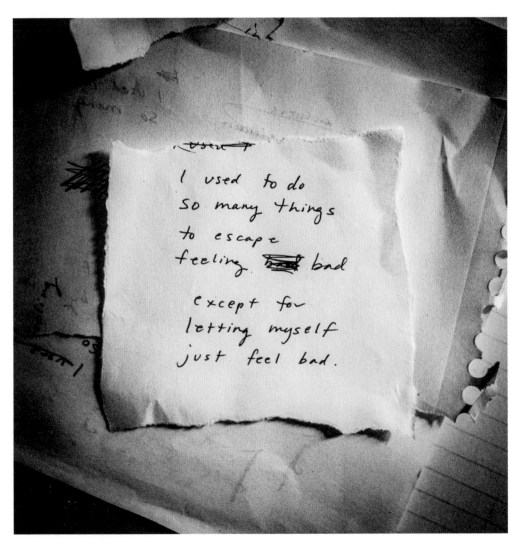

Emotion skills
are
relationship skills.

Everyone's practicing.

Feeling strong emotions is
scary if you
~~th~~ grew up in
a family that didn't
talk about them
like that's what
you do.
But talking about feelings
with each other is
just a skill.
You can always start
practicing now.

to know
what I need

I have to know
how I feel
to know
what I need

→

Feelings
Examples:

sad
overwhelmed
Lonely
Irritable
Tired
Hungry
Scared
Bored

Needs
Examples:

cry
downtime
talk to someone
solitude
rest
cake
help
play

Confusion about
how I feel =
confusion about
what I need

→ ?

?

Shame about
how I feel =
shame about
what I need

→ Me

Me

I feel so much better just
talking it out with
someone who says,
without words,

"I'm not going anywhere."

No wonder you think your job is to

Cheer people up, calm them down, or stay out of their way

if that's exactly what you had to do as a kid to feel safe.

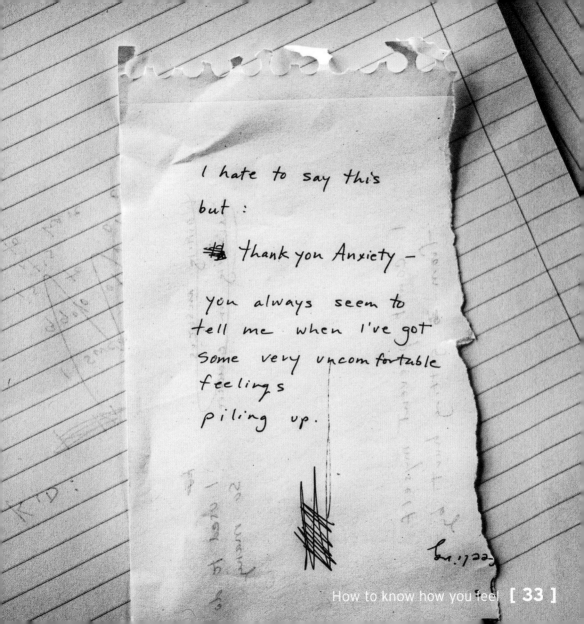

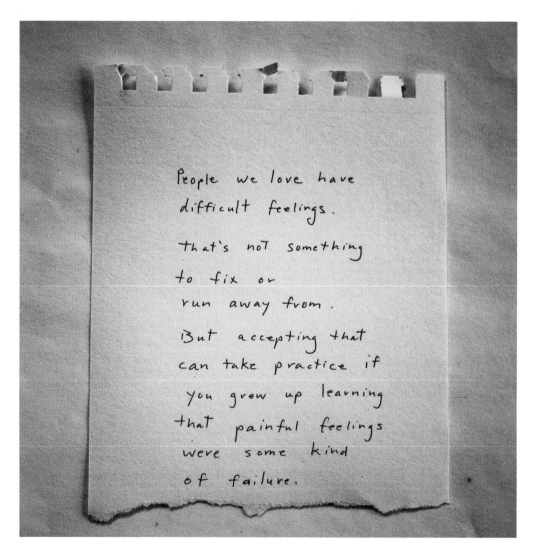

People we love have difficult feelings.

that's not something to fix or run away from.

But accepting that can take practice if you grew up learning that painful feelings were some kind of failure.

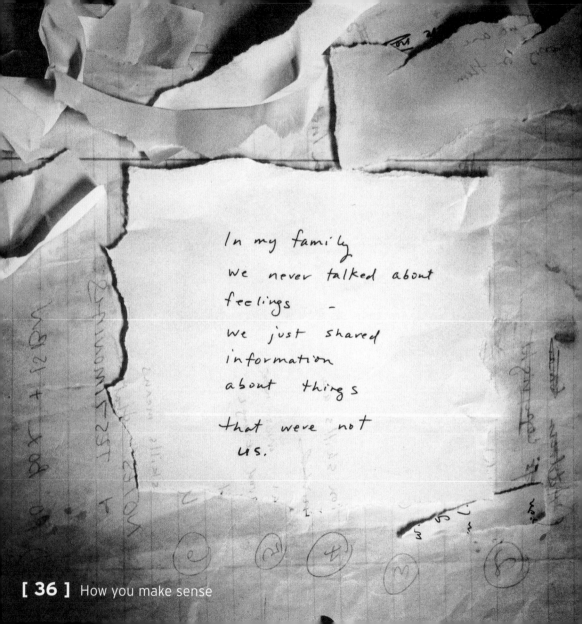

In my family
we never talked about
feelings –
we just shared
information
about things

that were not
us.

There are times I wish
someone would ask,
"What's that been like
for you?"
and then accept:
<u>That</u>'s what it's been like
for me.

How

You

Make

Sense

The reason therapists ask so much about childhood is because families are the original template for how people come to think life and relationships work. Were our parents happy? Were they angry? How did they talk to each other? How did they feel about being in a relationship, and how did their boundaries work?

When we struggle as adults, it's often because the skills that helped us survive the difficulties of childhood aren't actually helping us anymore.

You might, for example, have learned to get your parents' approval by being very helpful, quiet, or mature or getting good grades. Or maybe by helping them calm down or cheer up. Perhaps your parents even scared or overwhelmed you sometimes, so you learned to stay well out of their way.

As adults, we may find ourselves behaving in ways we don't

understand—or stuck in a relationship, frustrated at work, or feeling bad about ourselves. We might find it really hard to change, even though we want to. That feeling of helplessness to change can fill us with shame, sadness, anger, or guilt. But the truth of why we do what we do—as puzzling and painful as it may seem on the outside—nearly always begins to make sense when we look a little closer.

It's not a mystery, really. Mostly we're still doing what we did growing up. Humans evolved as a highly social species, and as children our primary needs are to be safe and to belong. So we will do whatever that takes. The strategies we learned as kids made us feel safe, and were so effective that we got a lot of repetition and practice. Usually about eighteen years' worth.

The past is wired right into our bodies. Right into our memory and nervous system. This helps protect us by preserving the memories of the things that caused us pain and how we responded. Often these impulses are on autopilot.

Once you start to unravel the past and make sense of some of the challenges you dealt with and the ways you learned to cope, you have more freedom to choose how to respond now. You don't have to be perfect, please everyone, fix other people's difficult emotions, or hide what you need. You can experiment with and practice new ways of communicating and behaving in order to get your needs met—you are not limited to only the tools you had as a little kid. Although a part of you will always be that child with those experiences, your present-day self is allowed to make any changes you want.

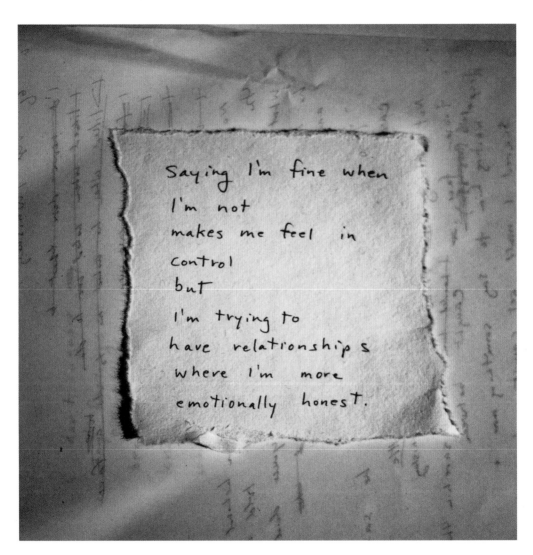

I don't always understand
healing . It doesn't seem
linear at all .

Sometimes I think
I'm stronger and
then —
an old wound starts
hurting again

reminding me that there
are some things I
will never be
over.

You're not supposed to
ignore
how you feel.

Your nervous system
evolved signals (aka
feelings)
for a reason:

to give you
feedback
on how you're doing +
what you need
in life.

I didn't know we could talk
about conflict.

I grew up watching people
s<u>top</u>
talking about things the
minute anyone got upset or
started to disagree.

Yes, it's uncomfortable.
But that's okay.

I think most people wish
they could be more of
who they are
and still feel accepted.

But it's understandably
hard if, growing up,
you were ignored or
shamed for being
yourself +
rewarded when you
conformed.

Some days I'm not
okay
and I'm not trying to
fix that.

No I don't need
advice on how
to _not_ feel
this way.

I just need time
to feel it.

I find it
stressful to
be around
people who insist
that everyone be
happy
all the time.

Growing up required
to obey —
and not trust what
I wanted or how
I felt —

Set ~~up~~ me up to be
an adult whose
default is to do
what others want me to

when I shouldn·t.

That really hasn·t been
good for me.

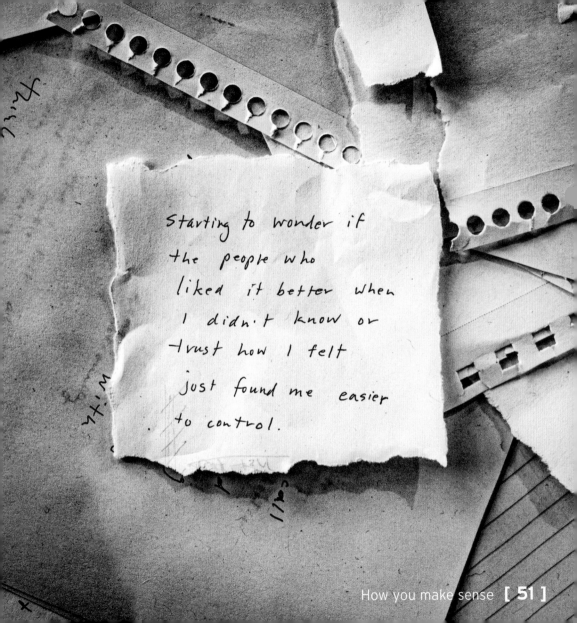

Starting to wonder if
the people who
liked it better when
I didn't know or
trust how I felt

just found me easier
to control.

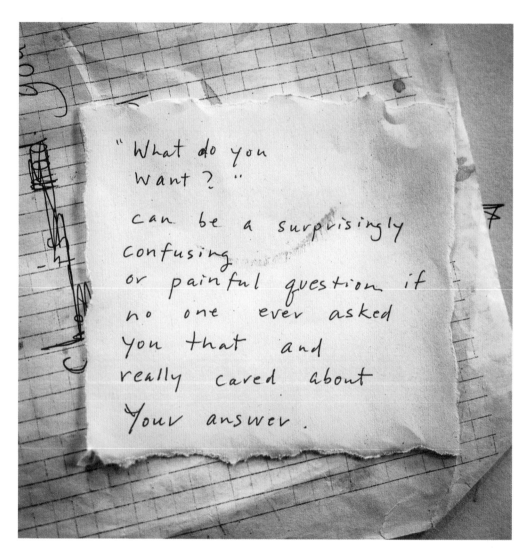

How you make sense

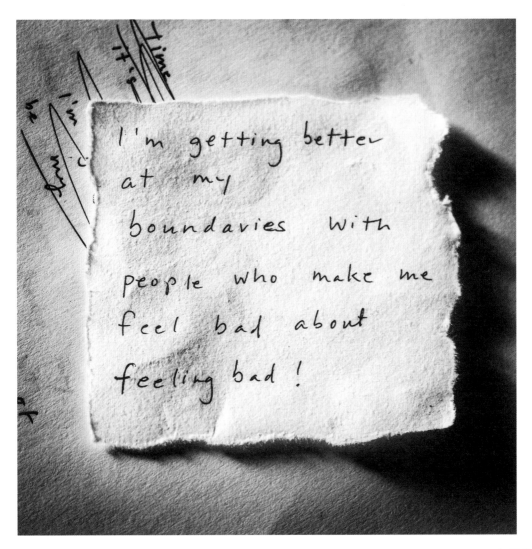

Someone I love gets
uncomfortable when
I feel _____.

But it's okay if
Someone I love
feels uncomfortable.

(I don't have to save
them from a
feeling.)

I can tell I'm not
really listening to you
if I'm already

planning my response
in my head.

If you grow up
having to be
vigilant
about adult emotions

it teaches you that

your job is

to prevent

or fix

everyone's uncomfortable
~~fee~~lings.

I guess it
makes sense that
people who have a
hard time with
my feelings

probably
also have a
hard time with
their own.

Disagreeing with someone you love doesn't mean you're wrong.

It just means that you've separate people.

Which is okay.

It's really hard, but
I've had to let myself
literally grieve
for a while about
how little power I
actually have

to change some
situations + relationships.

Before
I can know what I
need to do next.

the difference!

| FEELINGS | THOUGHTS |

(true, changeable, come + go, Adjectives)

(opinions, beliefs, ideas, information, Subjective, Arguable)

Examples —

" I feel : "
sad
excited
irritated
overwhelmed
hopeful
betrayed
uncertain
confused
scared
content

Examples —

"You're always ... "

"This won·t work. "

" He's jealous . "

" people aren·t there for me. "

" I know I can do this."

TRICK ONE !!
↓ ↓ ↓

" I feel like you are unreliable . "

(putting " I feel like "

in front of a thought doesn·t make it a feeling ! The real feeling might be "hurt," "betrayed", etc.)

How
to Know
How
You Feel

Having a relationship with your own feelings might be the most important relationship to have.

When you were a little kid, you didn't wonder how you felt. You just knew. You were in harmony with how you felt because your feelings were in your body, just like every other child, with a nervous system sending signals and feelings to you. Feelings gave you feedback on how you were doing or what you needed in life—essential information about your physical and emotional states of being.

Until you started to interact with the world.

Sometimes as you grow up, you learn that some of your feelings—or a lot of your feelings, maybe even all of your feelings—aren't acceptable to others. Or in certain environments. Maybe your feelings aren't welcome to people you love.

And so, because humans have a deep and physiological need to belong, we start to shape ourselves around these outside requirements. We start to avoid feelings that make other people uncomfortable. We lose our childhood ability to tune in easily to how we feel, to process those feelings, and move on.

When we shut down certain feelings, it's easy to lose our natural relationship with them. *But having feelings is an essential part of being human.* They are the essence of who you are as a person, and without them it's hard to know important things about yourself like:

who you are,

what kind of relationships you want,

what you want to do for work or purpose,

what gives your life meaning.

All of these things require having access to your feelings, and if feelings get a bad rap, it's because people often don't know what to *do* with them. If you grew up watching people hurry to escape or distract themselves from the discomfort of painful emotions, you may not even know that it's okay to just sit and tune in to them for a minute. Very often there is nothing to do, except to stop long enough to simply register what you're feeling.

Children need adults to talk about feelings like that's an ordinary thing to do, and to also show us how they handle their own. When we don't get healthy role modeling on what to do with anger or sadness or hopelessness or loneliness, we turn into adults who don't know how to engage with those feelings. When those feelings rise up (because they can't be contained forever), they come out in ways that hurt and confuse us, or other people.

It's easy to start categorizing some feelings as "good" and some feelings as "bad," but all our feelings are important and serve a purpose, no matter how uncomfortable. Even anger, sadness, and grief help us grow and process our lives.

We need feelings as a compass to guide us. Not knowing how you feel makes you feel stuck in life: You don't know what you're doing, or why. Everything is such a mystery. Other people are mysteries. You're a mystery to yourself.

Getting back to that childhood orientation of knowing how you feel is just a matter of practice. We're all built to tune in to how we feel. Even if you don't remember how, all your feelings are still there waiting. As you develop the skill of tuning in and getting that feedback from inside (see page 69 and page 73 for how to do this), the more comfortable you become with feeling, and with other people's feelings. Continuing to grow your emotional skills is part of being human. As you work on this, you increase your emotional intelligence. These are some qualities of people with strong emotional intelligence:

1. They're not perfectionists.

2. They're self-aware.

3. They're empathic.

4. They have a wide emotional vocabulary.

5. They have a sense of humor about themselves.

6. They're curious about other people.

7. They take downtime.

8. They set boundaries.

9. They're gracious and assertive.

10. They're good judges of character, can read people, and tune in to motivations.

11. They practice patience and calm, and take time to process emotional reactions.

12. They have fun.

13. They are hard to offend.

14. They squash negative self-talk.

15. They embrace change.

Feelings Are
Just Your
Body Talking
to You

One day I was googling some articles on breathing techniques for a client who was having a lot of anxiety. They all seemed too complicated, like how to count while breathing or whether to inhale with your mouth or nose. I knew that I, at least, would never remember any of those things in the middle of an anxiety attack. But then I saw an article that gave only one simple thing to do: *"Notice your breathing."* Now *that* I could remember. *"You don't have to **do** anything,"* it said.

Huh. I tried it immediately.

Two things I noticed: One, I was barely breathing. And then two, as soon as I paid attention, my body took a deep breath, unprompted.

I randomly started noticing my breathing in the car at red lights. Or waiting in a coffeeshop line. Almost always the first thing I noticed was how shallow my breathing was. But I also started noticing other things I didn't normally pay attention to, like my shoulders, which were so often up around my neck. Or that my stomach was nervous. (Had I had too much coffee already? Was I mulling over a conversation I had to have later?) Then my deep breath happened, and my shoulders dropped by themselves.

The simple act of noticing . . . well, it changes things.

Noticing is really the most basic form of mindfulness. Psychologist Ellen Langer at Harvard has been researching for decades how actively noticing new things around you puts you into a more present state of awareness in life. Skip the meditation, she says, and simply go straight to a state of mindfulness by being curious: As she says, *"Mindfulness isn't much harder than mindlessness."*

As I started expanding on this little skill of tuning in to my breathing, I started noticing emotions (and other sensations) more, my own and other people's. I started noticing more of what was happening around me. I noticed when I was tired. Hungry. Overwhelmed. Uneasy. Happy. Irritable. Sad. I noticed my feelings changing. Often quickly. (The bio major in me loves that feelings are physiological messages, aka interoception—very simply, messages from your brain tracking your body's physical and emotional state.)

With this feedback on how I was doing, I got better at taking care of myself. And I felt less like I had to control things, because I didn't have to anticipate everything: I could just notice things as they happened.

Feelings are just your body talking to you about how you're doing in the moment. Even if you've gotten used to ignoring them, they're still talking to you. Tune in to your breathing, and then your body, and then your emotions. It's a little thing that pays off big.

How to Feel Your Feelings in Five Steps

1. SLOW DOWN: Take a moment. At your desk, in the shower, sitting in your car at a light, or lying in bed. It can be almost anywhere.

2. TUNE IN TO YOUR BODY: All your feelings are in your body. Just like hunger, fatigue, and chilliness, your emotions create sensations, too. Turn your attention inward, and notice what you feel and where. Tense shoulders, chills, butterflies in your stomach, flushed face, emptiness, shallow breathing, and pain in your heart are some examples.

3. JUST NOTICE: Be loving, patient, and interested. You're not hurrying, analyzing, or judging the feeling right or wrong. Don't try to change it—just notice the way it feels and rest your attention there.

4. GIVE IT A MINUTE: Stay with the feeling long enough for you to accept its presence and for your brain to say "message received." You may be able to name the feeling now (sadness, loneliness, grief, etc.) or it may be hard to describe in words. That's okay. And trust when you want to stop.

5. KNOW THAT FEELINGS COME AND GO: Feeling an emotion doesn't mean you're done with it! Excitement, anxiety, joy, sadness, anger, love . . . they may be ongoing, or come back another time. It's okay to be nervous, but you won't actually die from your feelings! You can handle them all—in fact you were born for it.

When you are
upset + I am
too defensive to
listen,

it's because I'm
still learning that
it's okay for
people to feel
upset with me

and not have that
mean I'm a
bad person.

Boundaries are only
me making
it clear

This is okay with me.

This is not.

How I feel in all
my relationships began to
to change when I
had this idea :

What if I just
let myself listen
sometimes

without thinking
" I have to hurry up +
make this go away. "

I have to constantly practice
not jumping
the second someone tells
me they want something &
feeling like it's an
emergency

which it was to me,
growing up.

People get worried + say

"Well, if I let myself
feel _____
(sad, angry, overwhelmed, etc.)
then what will
I do?"

But it's okay to just
feel it + do
nothing else,
if you don't want to.

Feelings don't always
require ~~action~~.
action.

I object to the idea that
I wasn't born
lovable
but that I had to
work hard +
fix myself
to earn love.

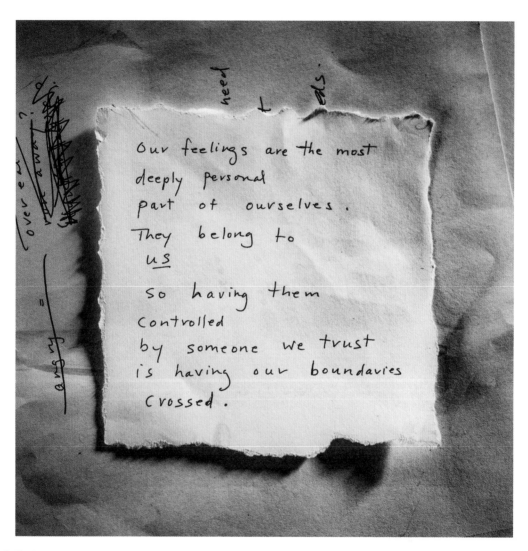

Our feelings are the most
deeply personal
part of ourselves.
They belong to
u<u>s</u>

So having them
controlled
by someone we trust
is having our boundaries
crossed.

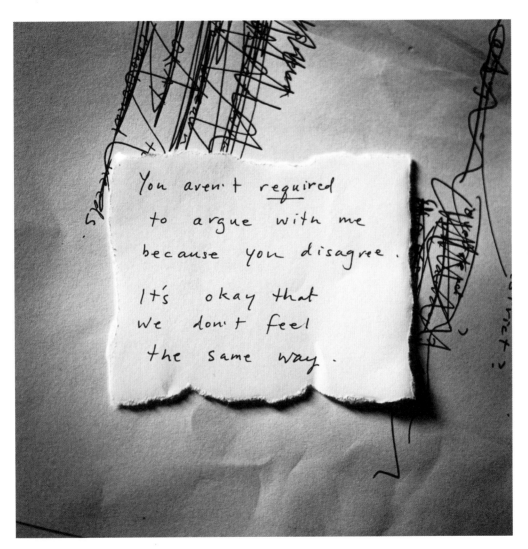

The main problem was
thinking I wasn't
supposed to
feel bad.

(People feel bad.
There's no need to
fix that.)

I get scared.

It's no
big deal.

I have to be
= the one to
make sure

I'm not treated
like my feelings
don't matter.

It's hard to know
how to deal with
conflict or
intense emotions
if you grew up with
adults who
couldn't handle it
themselves — so
they
~~so~~ didn't show
you how.

Emotion skills are
learned from watching +
practicing.

(But sometimes we got
more practice in
placating, anger, blame,
or shutting down.)

When I started changing
into a person who
wanted to take
better ~~doing~~ care of
me

there was some sadness
in noticing
who in my life didn't
like that.

Person 1 :   I'm hurting.

Person 2 :   Just don't think
              about it.

Person 1's
nervous system : < Not a chance. >

It's hard to grow up with
adults who can't
help you handle
your emotions because
they have no idea
how to handle
their own.

If someone shames me
for my feelings
or refuses to
listen –

I need to remember that
my emotional needs
aren't bad for me, but

the relationship
might be.

Sometimes the things
I grieve were
So important
it surprises me
how much they still
hurt –

and why wouldn't
they?

Pretty sure I have
a feelings
hangover.

I wish I hadn't been
taught that   it was
my job
to make people happy
all the time

instead of that.
people are allowed to
feel
   not happy.

It was seriously a
new concept for me
to learn that I could
just listen
to what someone is
upset about
and not be working
on my defense
instead.

I know that feeling.
Trying to control everything +
other people.

It's left over from
being a scared kid
with unhappy parents
who couldn't rescue
themselves.

So I tried to
do it
for them.

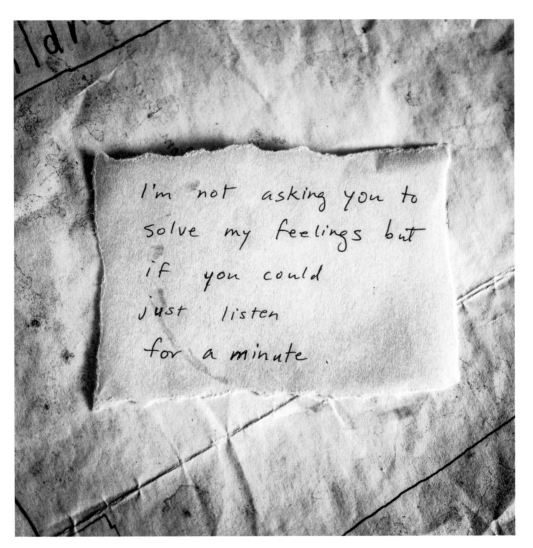

Relationships

Human beings are a highly social species with a long evolution that makes us desire both autonomy and connection. We need to grow and express our individuality freely—and at the same time, feel like we have people to rely on to love us and have our backs.

Our family is our very first relationship in life and the model, even into adulthood, for how we think relationships work. When we're secure in childhood, we grow up comfortable with having our needs met and also feel good about letting other people need us.

Important relationship skills include how to communicate our feelings, listen to others, deal calmly with conflict, and set boundaries for how we're treated. But we're not born with these skills. Children have brains that are super-smart, and they learn from watching—and copying—how the people around them do these things. That's a big part of what childhood is for.

But so often kids just have to obey what adults tell them to do or play the roles they figured out in order to cope with their family situation. Sometimes the adults we depend on have immature relationships skills themselves. Our parents might love us ... but they may not be the best teachers. And we may pick up ways of relating to others that serve us well as children but later on cause us, and others, a lot of distress.

One of the biggest relationship issues people have is with boundaries. Good boundaries are about letting ourselves and the people we love be separate from each other, with separate feelings, thoughts, and needs. Boundaries also refer to how we are treated by others: what's okay with us and what isn't.

If you grew up in a family that struggled with boundaries—in which people controlled or overwhelmed others, or in which children had the role of taking care of adults' needs—it can be hard to know where your boundaries start and stop or what's appropriate behavior. You might be worried about too much closeness, or too much distance, in relationships. But good boundaries aren't too rigid or too soft. They're flexible enough to change in different situations, or depending on how you feel.

The good news: We can start practicing new skills in life anytime we want. Here are some examples of things I'm always practicing:

1. How to say what I mean, as simply as possible, and not make people guess (even if I think they should).

2. How to reach out when I want to shut down.

3. How to just let myself *feel* sad, lonely, confused, a mess, when I would rather *do this thing I always do* and check out.

4. How to not be impatient or careless with the feelings of people I love.

5. How to listen and not try to solve someone else's problems.

6. How to take a break when I'm overwhelmed, and promise to return to the conversation a little later.

There's a personality trait called "openness to experience." Children have it. And we can rediscover it as adults with practice, by learning to be more emotionally open. People who are curious and open to experience literally see the world differently. Learning to be more accepting about your own emotional life leads to more acceptance with the emotions of others. And that leads to deeper, closer, more intimate connections. Which is something we all really need.

No wonder you
feel like everyone's
problems & hard feelings
are something you
have to fix ~~this~~

if that's exactly
what you had to do
as a kid.

I'm allowed to
grieve
relationships +
things
I can·t fix.

Me , when I'm hurting :

I do NOT
want to
talk about it
so don't
bring it up !

→

Why does
no one
even care
how I'm
doing ??

←

I sometimes get a little overwhelmed by change and need some time to emotionally catch up.

Always being rushed and
not knowing what
was going on as
a kid
overwhelmed my
nervous system and
made me feel unsafe
and that life was
scary and
out of control.

To get back to
the person I am
I had to reject
so much
of who I was
<u>told</u> that
I was.

I used to feel so
invisible
as a kid.

Now it's me who
has to stop acting
in relationships like
I am invisible
still.

Growing up never
being allowed to
say no
or disappoint an adult
in any way
meant that
when I left home I had
zero practice
setting boundaries or
handling someone being
upset with me.

I still get nervous about
conflict —
my big fear is things
escalating too fast.

So now I practice
setting limits & ~~letting~~
letting myself take
a break when I'm
overwhelmed.

I don't need to ask
permission
to do that.

when I watch someone
habitually shame
other people

I know I'm watching
a child who was

deeply controlled by
shame.

(I recognize that
distress
anywhere.)

Probably my
entire relationship to
grief + things that
happened long ago
can be
summed up as:

Sometimes I remember.
Sometimes I forget.

I'm not so sure
that emotionally
we ever leave
home for good.

I can actually just
practice

the skill of
talking about hard things.

(I mean , I've had to
practice doing a
lot of other
hard things.)

Still trying to
remind myself that
it's okay
to express feelings
that other people
don't want me
to.

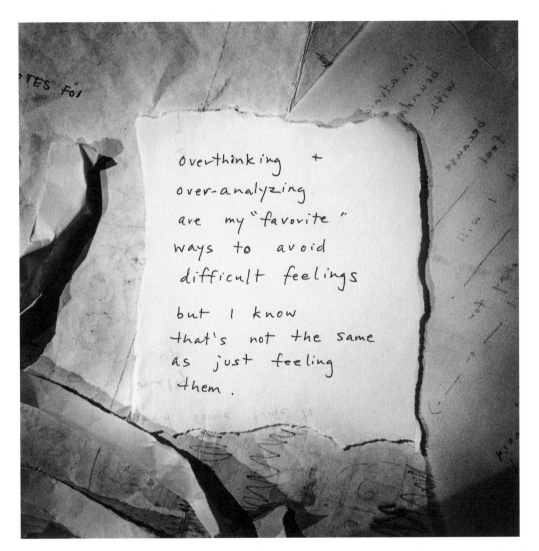

I'm afraid to set
boundaries
with _____

because they will
feel _____

and I will
feel _____ .

(But people are allowed
to feel ___ or ___ !)
(And you're allowed to
have
~~have~~ boundaries.)

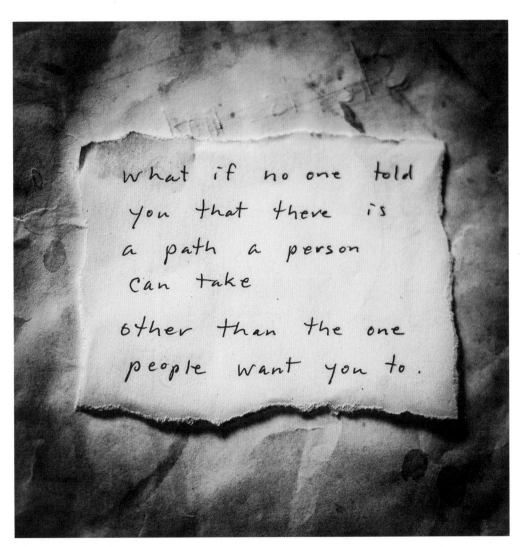

what if no one told
you that there is
a path a person
can take

other than the one
people want you to.

I often think peo
we're really seeking
one main thing:

people whose eyes,
when they see us,

light up with
delight.

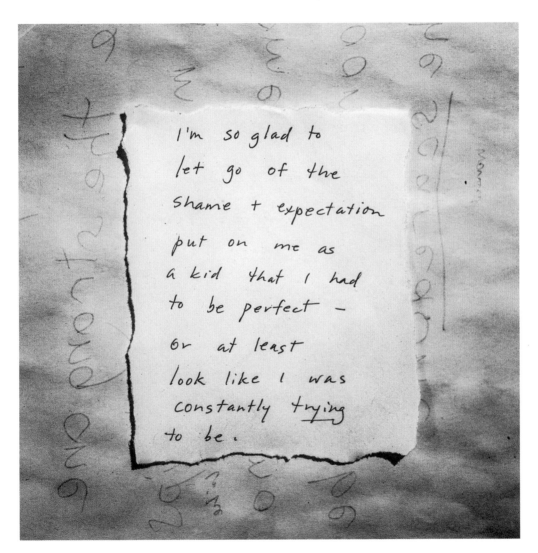

I'm so glad to
let go of the
shame + expectation
put on me as
a kid that I had
to be perfect —
or at least
look like I was
constantly trying
to be.

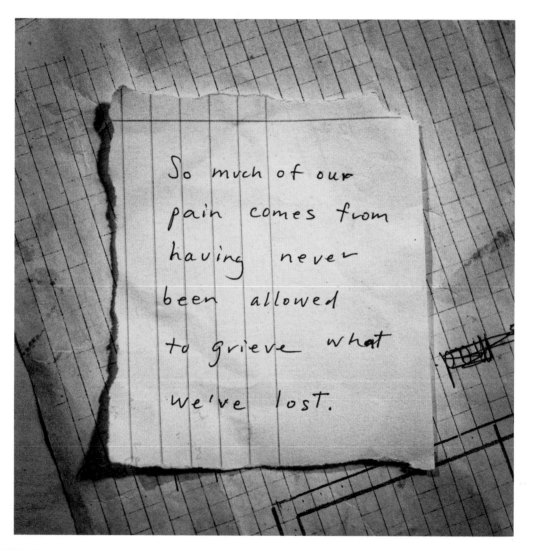

So much of our pain comes from having never been allowed to grieve what we've lost.

If I'm upset + I don't
understand why
someone is doing what
they're doing,
I could ask.

But I'd have to really
listen <u>really</u>, because
sometimes I get stuck
judging, arguing +
shutting them down
instead

and that's why I don't
understand.

When I tell someone who
is hurting to
think positive
feel better,
be grateful,
etc.

it's not them who can't
handle feeling sad,

it's me.

All valuable life skills
take pr<u>acti</u>ce !

driving, cooking, working,
earning money , self-care ...
and relationships.

None of them are
things we are born knowing.

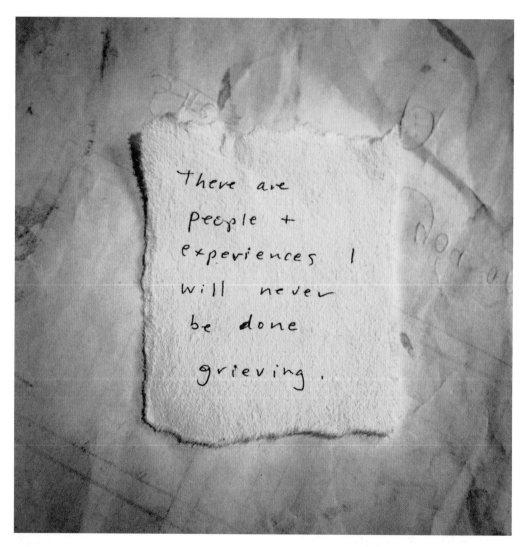

I'm still learning that
secure relationships
means

disconnecting +
reconnecting.

It's not over just
because we
fought.

Grief

My relationship with grief started when I was three and my mother died in a plane crash, shattering my whole family. We never spoke her name again, as if she'd never even been there. Years later, when my husband died in an accident, there was no possibility of shutting the pain behind closed doors. I was barely alive myself. But with children and a newborn baby I knew I couldn't put them through the confusing and dissonant silence that I had grown up with. I needed to grieve. And I needed help.

Friends who didn't know what to do or to say showed up, and then stayed—bringing us back to life with their presence.

Many years later, I see how that loss became the turning point of my whole life, bringing everything into sharper focus, stripping so much away, and putting my life's priorities into serious order.

No matter who you are, life is desperately hard sometimes. People we love die, and the longer we live, the more we find that's worth grieving. People we trust abandon us. Happy times come to an end. Circumstances change in ways that hurt us. Emotional needs go unmet. Trust gets broken. We are forced to let go of people, places, and things we loved dearly. There's even grief in letting go of who we thought we were.

Our culture is deeply nervous about grief. We think we're not supposed to feel pain about things that happen to us outside our control, and that it's best to *get over it* fast. We try to avoid or distract ourselves from despair to avoid feeling lingering pain—to put back on a mask of happiness, resilience, and equanimity as quickly as we can.

There's really no "polite" way to grieve. No way to control it once it has taken hold. And that scares people who are very nervous about losing control—of things, goals, other people, feelings, life. But how are we to numb ourselves against being hurt, without also numbing the part of us that craves to be fully alive?

We could use a better relationship with grief.

As a therapist who specializes in emotional pain, I can't think of one person who has walked through my door without some sort of grief standing in the way of healing what still hurts. There's something they just can't avoid anymore, though they've been trying very hard for a long time. They need someone to keep them company on a dark journey—to a place they often don't yet know they've been trying to go.

The emotional experience of grief touches all of our lives— from seemingly small losses that still ache to the catastrophic that reshape us completely, from top to bottom. Grief escapes wildly from our grasping control. And while it leaves scars upon us, it also imprints life more deeply with feeling and meaning. I plan to keep the conversation with grief going on my whole life, just the way I do with all my other emotions.

Grief has showed me that it's okay to ask for help, reach out to friends, talk about it, and learn how to let myself accept love, even though my world is upside down and I don't know what to do next. It's okay to need others. It's okay to let ourselves be affected by life and loss, and later acknowledge that even this overwhelming experience of grief didn't kill me.

We don't have to associate grief only with endings. When grief comes to sweep you away, tear you down, and reshape you . . . know that it's just the beginning—of a life reprioritized around more fully living.

As a kid
I felt like I
wasn't allowed to
have any emotional
or bodily
autonomy or privacy.

But somehow like magic
as an adult —

I was supposed to know
how good boundaries
work.

It's ridiculously hard sometimes

to be so human with such a fragile heart.

I still find it very
hard to
ask for help

So deep in my bones
is the lesson that
it's shameful if I
can't figure out
how to do everything
myself.

I can sometimes
find it hard to just
listen
when someone I love
is feeling upset + there's
nothing I can do about
it.

Because no one did that
for me growing up, so
I'm still learning

how that works.

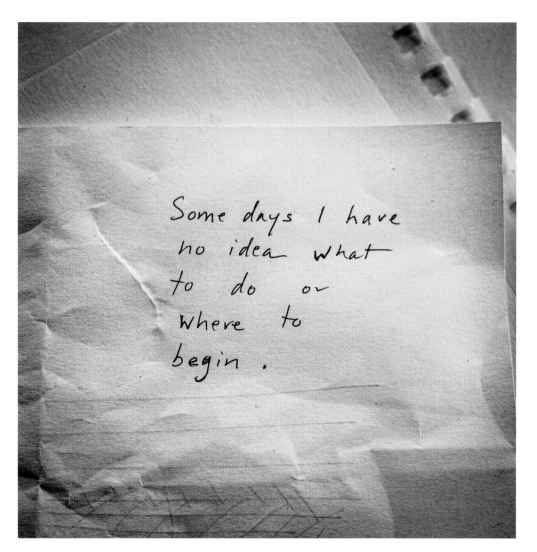

Some days I have
no idea what
to do or
where to
begin.

Being human means
experiencing trauma
of some kind or
another.
Big or small.

Thank goodness we're
also built to
recover
over time —
if we're not
abandoned, shamed,
or left alone to
cope with it
by ourselves.

How you make sense

It isn't being mean to have boundaries in relationships with people we love.

It just means letting people have separate feelings about things, and about what's okay with them & what isn't.

Your body produces signals —
aka feedback aka

FEELINGS !

↙ Physical State   ↘ Emotional State

hungry   happy
tired   sad
sleepy   mad
cold   scared
achy   excited
etc.   etc.

(You're supposed to
pay attention.)

(It's information, human biology +
a nervous system ⟶ telling you
how you're doing + what you need
in life!)

No Wonder
I was so afraid
of conflict —

it's not like I
grew up with
any experience

Watching people
make time
to work things out.

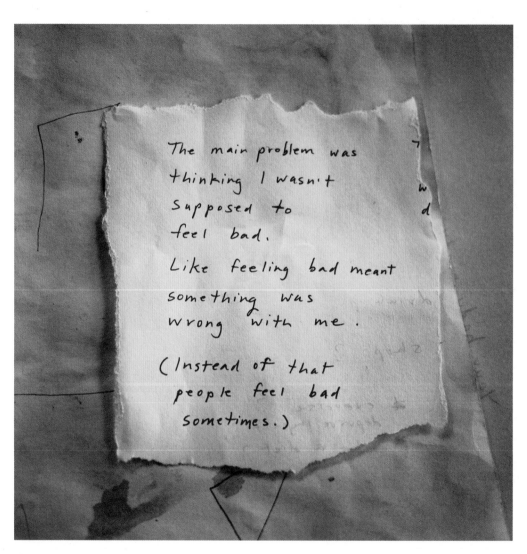

How to know how you feel

When you're an adult
the world likes to shame
you for having trouble with
boundaries + things like
that.

But as a kid
you were raised to put up
with whatever adults felt
like doing
and it wasn't like you
could say no.

A lot of us are doing
everything we can to
outrun old feelings of
sadness
because we're afraid
it will be

bottomless +
endless.

1. No, it's not bottomless.
2. No, it's not endless.
3. But yes, it might take
   a while.

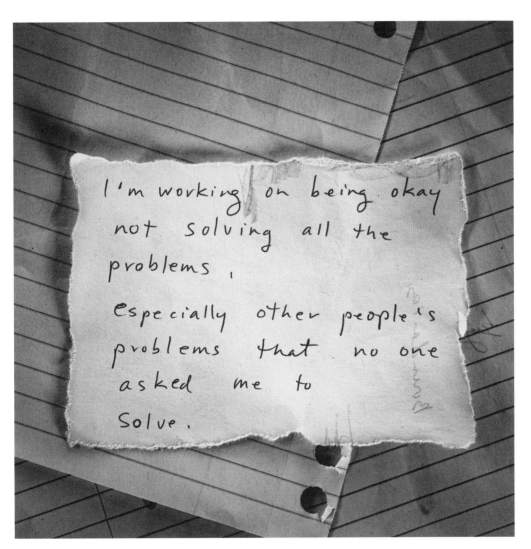

Being overly-focused on
other people's
feelings + moods + needs
(above your own) can
happen when that
was exactly the strategy
that kept you safe as
a kid.

Getting better at setting
boundaries has
mostly meant

me not
endlessly explaining
why I need them ~~it~~
to people who don't
like it.

(It's okay for them to
not like it.)

Do you think there's
something wrong
when someone you love
feels bad

or do you just
not know what to do
with their
emotions?

It's okay to
accept that
something
that happened to
you still
hurts

instead of trying
not to think
about it.

I haven't found
denial effective
for very
long.

We find ourselves
stuck in
certain relationships
so often

because our brains
prefer pattern +
what _feels_
familiar,

and have a blind spot
for what might be
new
and better for us
now.

I learned the
hard way :

You can't learn to
feel that you've
valued when

you've spending energy
on people who
don't find you
valuable.

Relationships can only get
so close if we
hide our vulnerability.

But deep connections are
built on
vulnerability.

So we might need to
unravel a little of what
we learned
growing up.

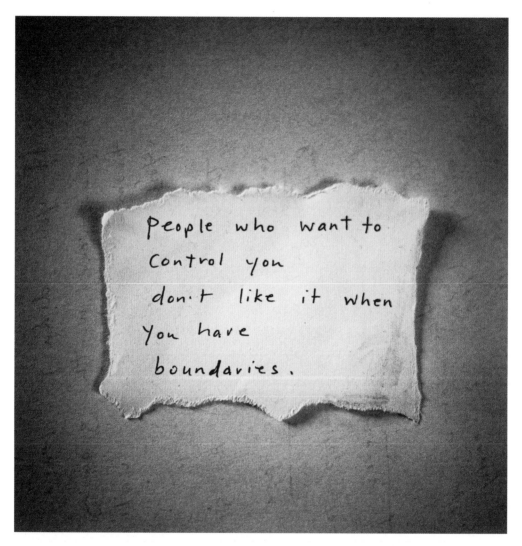

People who want to
Control you
don't like it when
You have
boundaries.

How to take good care of yourself

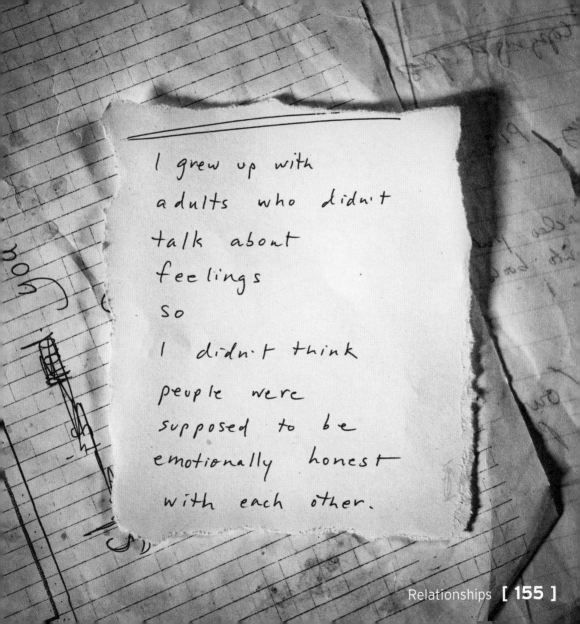

I grew up with
adults who didn't
talk about
feelings
so
I didn't think
people were
supposed to be
emotionally honest
with each other.

How to Take Good Care of Yourself

Many of us have absorbed messages about being driven or productive at all times. Or we might have internalized a need to be perfect, selfless, or to focus on others. For example, I grew up, as so many people do, with the idea that slowing down to enjoy life, play, rest, daydream, be outside, or meet friends to talk and hang out were not productive enough. The very idea of not being *productive* at all times was so frowned upon, it was no wonder I had to sneak off to the woods or hide with a book in a closet to daydream or do nothing. I declined then, and I decline now, the invitation to think of myself in such an economical or mechanistic way.

That's not my measure of a human being.

We don't have to pick up what others have laid down as true for us, and it's okay to live your life in a way that others don't accept or understand.

You may *want to* work, create, take care of your relationships, help others, and many other things. But none of that happens well if you don't have inner resources to draw on, and if you don't ensure that taking care of yourself is important—who will?

Choosing to take care of yourself *first* enables you to do all the things you want to in life, without resentment. Taking good care of yourself is the foundation on which all the other things must rest.

Taking good care of yourself includes:

1. knowing yourself, your feelings, and your values
2. listening to your body for when you need rest, solitude, play, or connection
3. having good boundaries with your feelings, relationships, time, and energy

4. being honest about who you are, your values, and what you
   want in life

5. letting yourself need others and ask for help

   One of my values is being strong and helping others. But it's
not helping others if I'm actually tired, miserable, or resentful.
I get to come first, even if others don't like it (and it's okay for
other people to not like it), and so do you.

If someone doesn't like it
when you put up boundaries
around how you'll be
treated —

it's okay for them to not
like it.

ably my
relationsh
vief t
appened
an be

(make sure to be)

~~It's okay to be~~

proud of

yourself
sometimes
for the ways

that you've

grown.

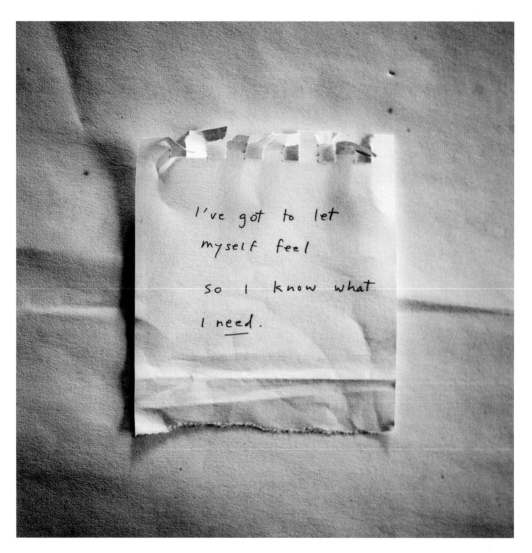

How to know how you feel

Letting ourselves
grieve

people, times,
relationships &
things we couldn't do
is part
of life.

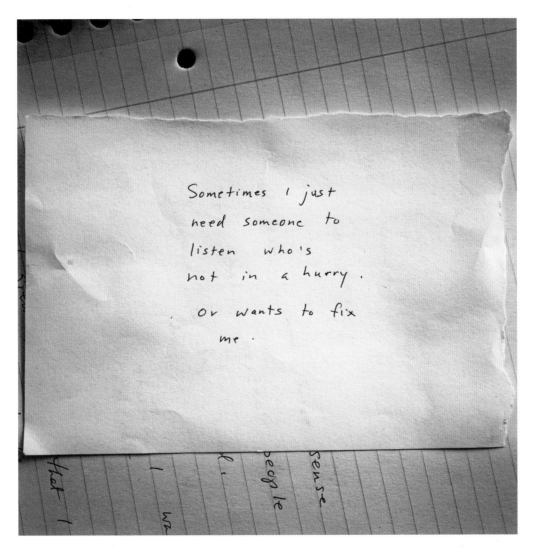

When you grow up +
your difficult feelings
are ignored, shamed,
or rejected

it makes sense that you

think you're not

lovable –

unless you're being

helpful, strong, "nice,"

independent, fearless,

or (something something something).

I try to

minimize

the amount of time
I spend around
people who would
like me better if

I weren't me.

That thing you avoid
because it makes
you emotional

might be the thing
you need to
talk about.

If you were a kid who
couldn't be upset, sad,
or scared without it
throwing adults into their
own intense feelings –

No wonder you have to
pretend you are always
okay.

You might not have
wanted it,
 but "apparently"
 you ~~are~~ were the one
with control over
whether other people
feel Good.

You hate being needy
but anyone who shamed
you for needing support,
safety, or love
was just in conflict with
their own neediness.

People are bu_il_t for
emotional needs —

it's what defines being

human.

You know what?

the thing about
emotion + relationship
skills   is —

they're just
SKILLS.

If no one showed us
before ,
the great thing is
we can learn them
now !
It's just practice,
that's all.

(Trial + error is
okay.)

It took a long time to
find out that
good relationships can
handle the natural
tendency that even
people who love each
other will disagree +
disconnect

and then need to
reconnect with each
other again.

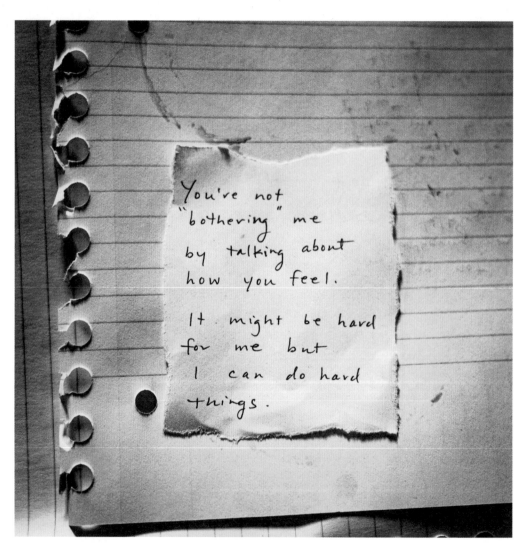

Being patient with
people I care about +
not rushing them
is also
being good to myself +
making a little
peace with
the past.

PERFECTIONISM:

You have to do everything right to be loved.

LOVE:

You don't have to do anything right to be loved.

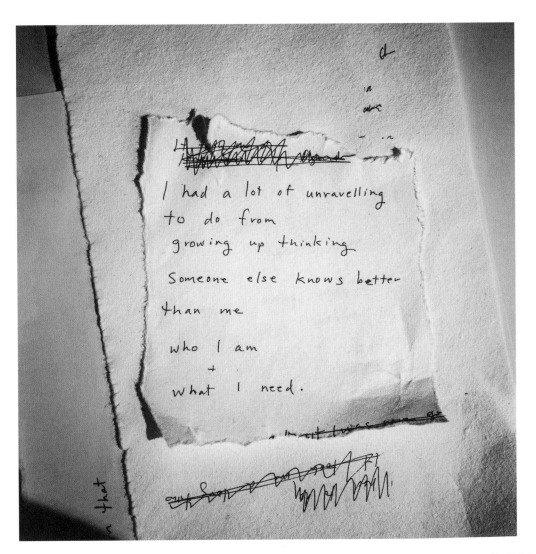

Don't let anyone shame you
for old feelings + fears
that come up again.
Old wounds will come up
again since they're in the
memory of your nervous
system +
the whole point
of your nervous system is
to keep you SAFE.
So it's going to remember
the painful + scary things
that happened to you.
Be kind to
yourself about that.

How to take good care of yourself

I needed to learn
that I can
listen to
the truth about
what it's like
being me,
right now.

Emotion + relationship skills are
just that — skills:

things we're not born knowing
how to do, but learn in
our relationships
(for better or worse).

there's no such thing as
"I'm bad at this. The end."
You can still practice
connecting, being vulnerable,
setting boundaries +
things like that
any time
you want.

Knowing yourself better &
trying to change things
is a process that
takes time &
practice so

don't be too hard on
yourself if
it doesn't happen

all at once.

- Saying you need more time
- Asking for help when you're overwhelmed by a "simple" task
- Taking a break to process strong feelings
- Asking not to be rushed...

These are just emotional self-care skills you might not have been taught — or allowed — growing up.

But you can teach yourself now if you want.

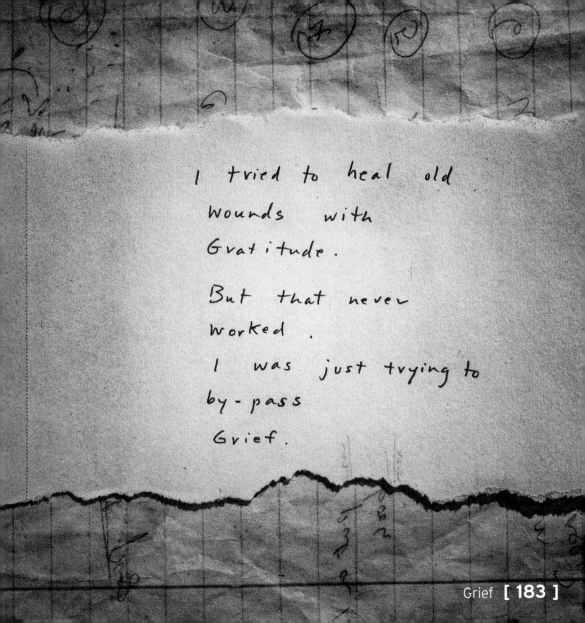

I tried to heal old
wounds with
Gratitude.

But that never
worked.
I was just trying to
by-pass
Grief.

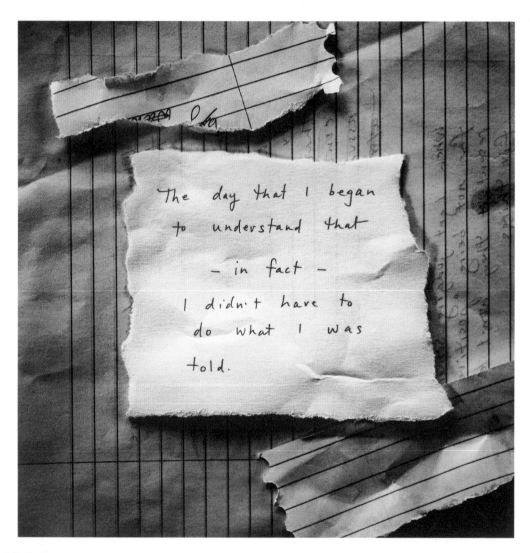

The day that I began
to understand that

- in fact -

I didn't have to
do what I was

told.

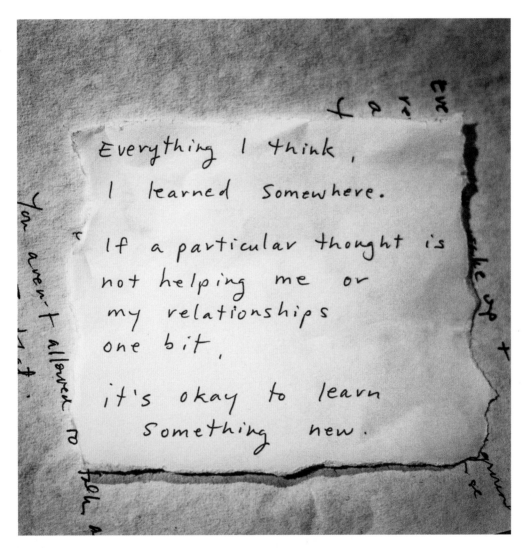

The best thing about
getting older is
giving in to ~~be~~
how desperately
I need ~~to be~~
~~to~~ live life on my
own terms.

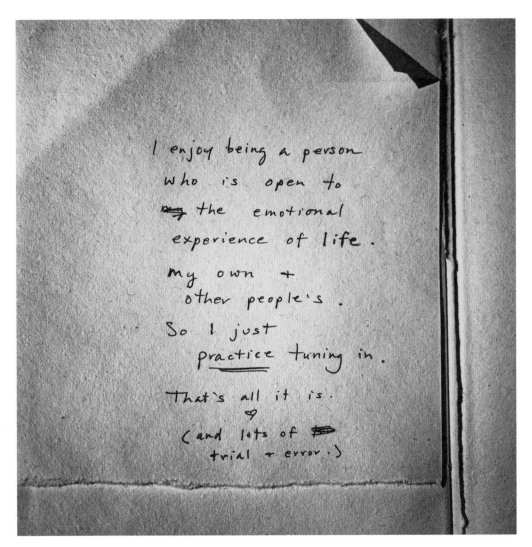

I enjoy being a person
who is open to
~~my~~ the emotional
experience of life.

My own +
other people's.

So I just
practice tuning in.

That's all it is.
♥
(and lots of ~~~~
trial + error.)

Wisdom

I don't know what wisdom is, but if I had to put it into words I would say that it's not a destination, but rather a lived experience over time, at the intersections and edges, with an openness to the emotional experience of life. Letting yourself reflect. Navigating hardship and grief. Wanting to know yourself deeply. Allowing yourself to be touched by life and other people. Welcoming what happens next. Nurturing curiosity, a sense of humor, and hope. Finding friends and companions along the way.

Maybe, before the end, I will learn to prioritize the most meaningful things, to keep myself rooted through the tearing winds of all the hard things that have happened, and those that are bound for me still—and all the extraordinary things that are happening or will come to happen, too.

To me, living is folding in the love and the grief with my desire for both perseverance and peace, and feeling mostly like I'm in harmony with life—knowing that I belong to life, and life belongs to me.

You're not here to
be perfect or to
set a good example
or to please anyone.

You were born to
love + enjoy
your ordinary,
peculiar, inconsistent,
good-enough self.

Acknowledgments

There is no creativity for me without connection. I want to thank:

My kids, for being the reason.
Rafe.
My Instagram community, for their vulnerability and authenticity.
Renée Zuckerbrot, my agent, for believing in me.
Stephanie Fletcher, my editor, for her thoughtful and spot-on guidance.
My mother.
Jane, for doing double-duty with a commitment to making creative dreams real.
The Wednesday Writers.
Anne, for art, laughter, and risk.
Robin, Lorimer, Martha, Helena, Jeff, Tiffany, Mary, Kiki, Maribeth, Annie, and Nancy.
My clients, who teach me about courage.
Ed and Renee, the Widows Club.
Doug, for the joy and love.
Sonia and Mickey, for rooting for me.
Everyone who's ever been real with me, and let me be real.